Non-Traditional Hat Patterns

6 Crochet Hat Patterns

by:
Christina Williams
Craft Bindings

Table of Contents

A Rather Festive Hat   2
Pickelhaube   8
Wizardry   13
Team Captain   17
Tyrant Helm   23
Nappers Respite   31

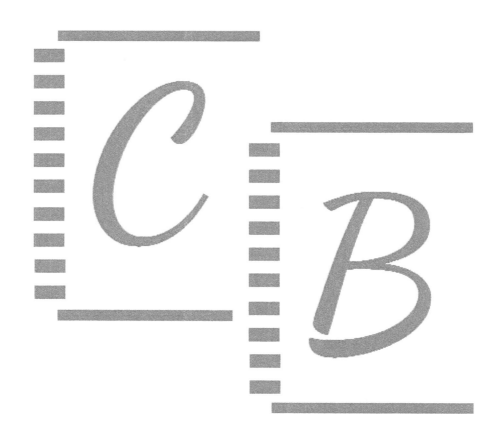

A Rather Festive Hat

Materials needed:
size H (5 mm) crochet hook
Worsted weight yarn (I used Red Heart) in:
green - about 200 yards
white - about 25 yards
yellow - 5 yards
and about 2 yards each of red, blue and black.
a tapestry needle

Gauge:
4 sts + 4 rows = 1 inch

Measurements:
This hat is 24 inches around at the base and 13 inches tall.

Abbreviations:
sc - single crochet
dc - double crochet
ch - chain
sts - stitches
sc2tog - single crochet 2 together

Stitches used:
chain
single crochet
front post single crochet (single crochet around the stitch, not through top bars)
double crochet

Notes:
This hat is worked from the bottom up, in the round without an attaching stitch. The base is worked first and the trim and ornaments are attached later on. The base chain in round one can be started using regular chain stitches or single crochet base chain.

With white yarn:
either : rnd1 - ch 72, join, rnd 2 - single crochet 72 around.
or : rnd 1 - single crochet base chain 72, join.
Starting rnd 1: sc 72 around, place marker to mark your starting stitch. (this is just for accuracy and stitch count)
rnd 2 - 8: sc 72 around.

Switch to green and begin increase with post stitches:
rnd 9: 2 front post single crochets around the fist stitch, 11 front post single crochet, (2 front post single crochets around the next stitch, 11 front post single crochets) 5 more times. (78 sts)
*This row makes the bottom of the tree stick out right away without having a curve.
rnd 10: 2 single crochets in the first stitch, sc 12, (2 sc, sc 12) 5 times. (84 sts)
rnd 11: 2 single crochets in the first stitch, sc 13, (2 sc, sc 13) 5 times. (90 sts)
rnd 12: sc 90.

Begin decrease:
rnd 13: (sc2tog, sc 13)6 times. (84 sts)
rnd 14: sc 84
rnd 15: (sc2tog, sc 12)6 times. (78 sts)
rnd 16: sc 78
rnd 17: (sc2tog, sc 11)6 times. (72 sts)
rnd 18: sc 72
rnd 19: (sc2tog, sc 10)6 times. (66 sts)
rnd 20: sc 66
rnd 21: (sc2tog, sc 9)6 times. (60 sts)
rnd 22: sc 60
rnd 23: (sc2tog, sc 8)6 times. (54 sts)
rnd 24: sc 54
rnd 25: (sc2tog, sc 7)6 times. (48 sts)
rnd 26: sc 48
rnd 27: (sc2tog, sc 6)6 times. (42 sts)

rnd 28: sc 42

Begin increase for second section:
rnd 29: 2 front post single crochets around the first stitch, front post single crochet 6, (2 front
post single crochets, front post single crochet 6) 5 more times. (48 sts)
rnd 30: (2 sc, sc 7) 6 times. (54 sts)
rnd 31: (2 sc, sc 8) 6 times. (60 sts)
rnd 32: sc 60

Begin decrease:
rnd 33: (sc2tog, sc 8) 6 times. (54 sts)
rnd 34: sc 54
rnd 35: (sc2tog, sc 7) 6 times. (48 sts)
rnd 36: sc 48
rnd 37: (sc2tog, sc 6) 6 times. (42 sts)
rnd 38: sc 42
rnd 39: (sc2tog, sc 7) 6 times. (36 sts)
rnd 40: sc 36
rnd 41: (sc2tog, sc 6) 6 times. (30 sts)
rnd 42: sc 30
rnd 43: (sc2tog, sc 5) 6 times. (24 sts)
rnd 44: sc 24
rnd 45: (sc2tog, sc 4) 6 times. (18 sts)
rnd 46: sc 18

Begin increase:
rnd 47: 2 front post single crochets around the first stitch, front post single crochet 2, (2 front
post single crochets, front post single crochet 2) 5 more times. (24 sts)
rnd 48: (2 sc, sc 3) 6 times. (30 sts)
rnd 49: sc 30

Begin decrease:
rnd 50: (sc2tog, sc 3) 6 times. (24 sts)

rnd 51: sc 24
rnd 52: (sc2tog, sc 2) 6 times. (18 sts)
rnd 53: sc 18
rnd 54: (sc2tog, sc 1) 6 times. (12 sts)
rnd 55: sc 12
rnd 56: sc2tog 6 times. (6 sts)
rnd 57: sc 6, fasten off leaving a 12 inch tail.
weave the yarn tail through the last 6 stitches, pull tight and tasten off. The base of the hat is done! Really you can decorate it however you'd like from here but I used crochet lights, bobbles (I call them) and garlan.

Lights: With colored yarn of your choice - chain 2, attach black and chain 2 then fasten off. Tie off the two center yarn tails from the color change then tie the two black yarn tails together and then the two color yarn tails together. Pull yarn tails through the hat and use them to tie it off.

Bobbles: With color of your choice - chain 2, double crochet into the first chain, double crochet around the last double crochet, turn. Pull the starting yarn tail up in front and around to the back so that the next stitch you make is made over it, double crochet into the starting chain. Fasten off by pulling both the working yarn and the yarn tail through the loop on your hook. Use these tails to tie the bobble to your hat.

Garland: You can use any color you'd like, I used white -
1st - using the same method as single crochet base chain, double crochet base chain 75, fasten off. Pin this to the lower section of the tree and sew on. I just used a simple up and down through the center of the stitches with white yarn.
2nd - double crochet base chain 45, fasten off. Pin this to the second section of the tree and sew on in the same method as the last garland.

Star: rnd 1: using magic loop method, sc 6, pull center circle tight.
rnd 2: 2 sc in each sc around. (12 sts)

rnd 3: single crochet through the front post only twice, turn, single crochet through unused post of last stitch, single crochet through the unused post of the next stitch, turn. sc2tog, sc, fasten off.
reattach yarn into the 3rd stitch of rnd 2 - sc front post only, twice. turn. sc using unused post, twice, turn, sc2tog, sc, fasten off.
reattach yarn into the 5th stitch of rnd 2 - sc front post only, twice. turn. sc using unused post, twice, turn, sc2tog, sc, fasten off.
reattach yarn into the 7th stitch of rnd 2 - sc front post only, three times. turn. sc using unused post, three times, turn, single crochet 3 together, sc, fasten off.
reattach yarn into the 10th stitch of rnd 2 - sc front post only, three times. turn. sc using unused post, three times, turn, single crochet 3 together, sc, fasten off.
It looks like that's a lot of ends to hide and you're right, it is. I just took the tail from attaching the new yarn and pulled it up through the star points and cut it and took the tails from the ends of the tail points and pulled them down through and cut it. Use a simple stitch to attach the star to the very tip of your hat.
You can make as many bobbles and lights and garlands as you'd like to decorate your tree! Then you can wear it out and show it off.

Pickelhaube

Materials:
5oz Worsted weight yarn in main color (for red- Red Heart, cherry red, for blue- Red
heart, Delft blue), 1oz worsted weight yarn in contrasting color (for red- Red Heart,
cornmeal, for blue- Red Heart, linen).
Size G or 4.25mm crochet hook
yarn needle

Gauge:
4 fpdc + 3 rows = 1 inch
Measurements:
This hat is 24" around at the base, 6" tall without the spike, and the spike is 5" tall.

Abbreviations:
ch- chain
slst- slip stitch
blo- back loop only
sc- single crochet
sc2tog- single crochet two together
st- stitch
rnd- round
fpdc- front post double crochet
bpdc- back post double crochet
fpsc- front post single crochet
bpsc- back post single crochet

Notes:
This hat is worked in a spiral (without joins) starting at the top of the hat. The spike is worked in rounds from the bottom up then sewn onto the hat. Starting in rnds and increasing every rnd by 6, with main color:

Rnd 1: Ch2, sc6 in second ch from hook.
Rnd 2: Place marker, (sc, fpdc around same st) around. (12 sts)

Rnd 3: (sc, fpdc around same st, fpdc) around. (18 sts)
Rnd 4: (sc, fpdc around same st, fpdc 2) around. (24 sts)
Rnd 5: (fpdc around sc, fpdc, sc on top of next st, fpdc around same st, fpdc) around. (30 sts)
Rnd 6: (fpdc 2, fpdc around sc, fpdc, sc on top of next st, fpdc around same st) around. (36 sts)
Rnd 7: (sc in top of next st, fpdc around same st, fpdc 5) around. (42 sts)
Rnd 8: (fpdc around sc, fpdc, sc in the top of next st, fpdc around same st, fpdc 4) around. (48 sts)
Rnd 9: (fpdc 2, fpdc around sc, fpdc, sc in top of next st, fpdc around same st, 3 fpdc)
around. (54 sts)
Rnd 10: (fpdc 4, fpdc around sc, fpdc, sc in the top of next st, fpdc around same st, fpdc 2) around. (60 sts)
Rnd 11: (fpdc 6, fpdc around sc, fpdc, sc in top of next st, fpdc around same st, fpdc)
around. (66 sts)
Rnd 12: (sc in top of next st, fpdc around same stitch, fpdc 7, fpdc around sc, fpdc 2)
around, (72 sts)
Rnd 13: (fpdc around sc, fpdc, sc in the top of next st, fpdc around same st, fpdc 9) around. (78 sts)
Rnd 14: (fpdc 2, fpdc around sc, fpdc, sc in the top of next st, fpdc around same st, fpdc 8) around. (84 sts)
End increasing.
Rnd 15-23: fpdc around.
At the end of rnd 23, after last fpdc, fpsc around next st, slst into next st, ch 1. This will be the start of the front brim. You will work the brim in rows.

Brim: With main color:
Row 1: fpdc 10, 2 fpdc over next st, fpdc 10, 2 fpdc over next st, fpdc 10, ch 1, turn. (34 sts)
Row 2: skip 1st st, bpdc over next st, bpdc to last two sts, 1 bpdc over the posts of the last two sts, ch 1, turn. (32 sts)

Row 3: skip 1st st, fpdc over next st, fpdc 8, 2 fpdc over next st, fpdc 10, 2 fpdc over next st, fpdc to last two sts, 1 fpdc around posts of the last two sts, ch 1, turn. (32 sts)

Row 4: skip 1st st, bpdc over next st, 1 bpdc around posts of the next two sts, bpdc to last four sts, (1 bpdc around post of next two sts) twice, ch 1, turn. (28 sts)

Row 5: skip 1st st, fpdc over next st, 1 fpdc over posts of the next two sts, fpdc 4, 2 fpdc in next st, fpdc 10, 2 fpdc in next st, fpdc 4, (1 fpdc over post of the next two sts) twice, ch 1, turn. (26 sts)

Row 6: skip 1st st, bpdc over next st, 1 bpdc over posts of the next two sts, bpdc to last 4 sts, (1 bpdc around post of the next two sts) twice, ch 1, turn. (22 sts)

Row 7: skip 1st st, fpdc around next st, 1 fpdc around posts of next two sts, fpdc to last 4 sts, (1 fpdc around posts of next two sts) twice. (18 sts)

Fasten off.

From the left side, lower corner (where it connects to the hat), skip 10 sts, attach yarn, ch1. Follow instructions for Brim Rows 1-7 again but DO NOT FASTEN OFF. There will be 10 sts between brims on either side of the hat. Sc around the bottom of the entire hat as follows: 12 sc evenly spaced down side of the brim, 10 sc along side of hat, 12 sc along side of the brim, 2 sc at corner of brim, 18 sc along top of brim, 2 sc in corner of brim, 12 sc along side of brim, 10 sc along the side of the hat, 12 sc along side of brim, 2 sc in corner of brim, 18 sc along top of brim, 2 sc in corner of brim, join with slst to 1st sc.

Top Point:

Working in rounds with joins and contrasting color. The first stitch of every rnd is worked in the same st as the slst.

Rnd 1: ch 24, join with slst into first ch, sc 24 around, join with slst to first sc, ch 1. (24 sts)

Rnd 2: sc blo this round, (sc 2, sc2tog) around, join with slst, ch 1. (18 sts)

Rnd 3: fpsc around, join, ch 1. (18 sts)

Rnd 4-5: sc around, join, ch 1. (18 sts)

Rnd 6: (2 fpsc, 2 fpsc around next st) around, join, ch 1. (24 sts)

Rnd 7: (sc 3, 2 sc in next st) around, join, ch 1. (30 sts)

Rnd 8: (sc 4, 2 sc in next st) around, join, ch 1. (36 sts)
Rnd 9: bpsc around, join, ch 1. (36 sts)
Rnd 10: (sc 2, sc2tog) around, join, ch 1. (27 sts)
Rnd 11: (sc 1, sc2tog) around, join, ch 1. (18 sts)
Rnd 12: (sc 2, sc2tog) around, join, ch 1. (12 sts)
Rnd 13-14: sc around, join, ch 1. (12 sts)
Rnd 15: (sc 4, sc2tog) around, join, ch 1. (10 sts)
Rnd 16-17: sc around, join, ch 1. (10 sts)
Rnd 18: (sc3, sc2tog) around, join, ch 1. (8 sts)
Rnd 19-20: sc around, join, ch 1.
Rnd 21: (sc 2, sc2tog) around, join, ch 1. (6 sts)
Rnd 22: sc around, join, ch 1. (6 sts)
Rnd 23: (sc, sc2tog) around, join, ch 1. (4 sts)
Rnd 24: sc 4, fasten off.

Thread yarn end through the yarn needle and pull yarn around the second stitch of the last rnd, from front to back, down through the center of the spike. Stuff spike as well as possible and sew to the center top of the hat, covering rnds 1-3 of the hat.

Strip around the hat: With contrasting color:

Ch 90, turn and work 100 single crochets around the chain, not working in any loops, slst in last ch. Fasten off, leaving at least 28 inches to sew this onto the hat.

Sew this strip around the bottom of the hat as straight as you can, going over the top of the brims.

Hide strings and enjoy!

Wizardry

Materials: 7 oz of Delft blue Red Heart worsted weight yarn for main color (mc)
1 oz of Yellow Red Heart worsted weight yarn for contrasting color (cc)
3 oz of black Red Heart worsted weight yarn for the belt.
Size H crochet hook
Yarn needle

Gauge: 4 rows and 4 single crochet = 1 inch

Measurements: 12 inches high, 2 inch wide brim, 22 inches around at the base.

Abbreviations:
sc – single crochet
ch – chain
rnd – round
st(s) – stitch(es)
fpsc – front post single crochet

Notes: This hat is worked from the top down in a spiral with no joins at the ends of the rounds. This hat is worked with the increases stacked on top of each other which gives it a swirled look. It looks like this from the top:
This was intentional, I think that it adds to the stability of the hat and I love it!

With mc using magic loop method – sc 4 in loop, pull tight.
Begin increasing 2 stitches every row in the first stitch of the round and the first stitch of the second half-
Rnd1: place a marker to mark the beginning of the round and move it up every row- 2 sc in the first st, sc, 2 sc in next st, sc.
Rnd 2: 2 sc in the first st, sc 2, 2 sc in the next st, sc 2.
Rnd 3: 2 sc in the first st, sc 3, 2 sc in the next st, sc 3.
Rnd 4: 2 sc in the first st, sc 4, 2 sc in the next st, sc 4.
Rnd 5: 2 sc in the first st, sc 5, 2 sc in the next st, sc 5.

Rnd 6-42: Continue increasing in the first stitch and the middle stitch until there are 88 sts total.

Brim:
Increasing by 8 stitches per round for the first 6 rounds-
Rnd 43: fpsc 11, sc in next sc, (fpsc around the post of the same stitch as last sc, fpsc 10, sc in next sc) around. (This gives the brim a nice solid turn while increasing, instead of a gradually increased brim.)
Rnd 44: sc 6, 2 sc in next sc, (sc 11, 2 sc in next st) 7 times, sc to end.
Rnd 45: sc 3, 2 sc in next sc, (sc 12, 2 sc in next st) 7 times, sc to end.
Rnd 46: (sc 13, 2 sc in next st) around.
Rnd 47: sc 9, 2 sc in next st, (sc 14, 2 sc in next st) 7 times, sc to end.
Rnd 48: sc 3, 2 sc in next st, (sc 15, 2 sc in next st) 7 times, sc to end.
Rnd 49: sc around, change to cc.
Rnd 50: sc around, fasten off.

Belt buckle:
With cc – ch 24, slip stitch to the first chain to form a loop.
Ch1, sc in the same stitch, sc 1, 3 sc in next ch, sc 5, 3 sc in next ch, sc 5, 3 sc in next ch, sc 5, 3 sc in last ch, sc 3, slip stitch to top of the first sc of the round.
Now you're going to work in rows on one single stitch to finish.
Row 1: Ch 1, sc in the same stitch as join, ch 1, turn.
Row 2: sc, ch 1, turn.
Row 3-8: repeat row 2, fasten off leaving at least a 6 inch tail for sewing this to the hat later on. From now on this will be called the buckle rod. :) (This should be just long enough to overlap the other side of the buckle.)

Belt:
With black yarn, working back and forth in row ch 7
Row 1: sc in 2nd ch from hook, sc across. (6 sc)
Row 2: sc across.
Row 3-84: sc across. (about 21 inches)
Row 85: sc 2, ch 2, skip center two stitches, sc in the last two stitches, ch 1, turn.

Row 86: sc 2, 2 sc in center ch space, sc 2, ch 1, turn.
Repeat (rows 85 and 86) 8 more times. Fasten off.

Sewing:
Place the beginning of your belt, the side that does not have the buckle holes, on the left side of the hat, about 2 inches in front of center, (toward the front). Sew into place along the chain stitches.
Place the end of the belt, right side up over the buckle and pull the buckle rod through the sixth hole from the end.
Wrap the belt around the base of the hat, make sure the belt buckle is flat and facing the right way and use the tail from the end of the buckle to sew it through the belt and the hat. I used two stitches for this part, one at each corner of the end of the buckle rod.

Optional:
Sew each corner of the buckle to the hat to ensure no movement.
Enjoy!

Team Captain

Materials:
5oz worsted weight yarn for main color
2oz worsted weight yarn in black
1oz worsted weight yarn in linen
size G or 4.25 mm crochet hook
yarn needle

Gauge:
5 rows and 4 sts = 1 inch

Abbreviations:
ch – chain
sc – single crochet
sc2tog – single crochet two together
fpdc – front post double crochet
st(s) – stitch(es)

Measurements:
(l)arge – 22", (m)edium – 20 1/2", (s)mall – 19" written into the pattern as l(m,s)

Notes: This hat is made starting with a triangle, starting from the bottom and decreasing to the top, then crocheted around to form the hat. The brim, emblem and buttons are made separately and sewn on.

To begin for all sizes and main color: ch 31,
Row 1: starting in the 2nd ch from hood, sc2tog, sc to last 2 chains, sc2tog, ch 1, turn.
Row 2: sc2tog, sc to last 2 sts, sc2tog.
Row 3-14: repeat row 2.
You should be left with 2 sts. Now we will single crochet around the first half of the
triangle then make our chain for the rest of the hat and then single crochet up the second side of the triangle and begin crocheting in a spiral (rounds without joins).

Rnd 1: sc2tog, sc 14 along the side of the triangle, ch 60(54,48), join with a slip stitch to the lower right hand corner of the triangle, sc 15 up the side of the triangle, place a
marker here and move it up with each round. Do not join or turn.
Rnd 2: (2 sc in next st, sc 14(13,12)) repeat around.
Rnd 3: (2 sc in next st, sc 15(14,13)) repeat around.
Rnd 4: remove marker, sc 3, place marker (moving your starting point over three
stitches), (2 sc in next st, sc 16(15,14)) repeat around.
Rnd 5: (2 sc in next st, sc 17(16,15)) repeat around.
Rnd 6: (2 sc in next st, sc 18(17,16)) repeat around.
Rnd 7: sc around.
Rnd 8: (sc2tog, sc 18(17,16)) repeat around.
Rnd 9: sc 3, (sc2tog, sc 17(16,15)) repeat 5 times total, sc2tog, sc 14(13,12).
Rnd 10: sc 6, (sc2tog, sc 16(15,14)) repeat 5 times total, sc2tog, sc 10(9,8).
Rnd 11: sc 9, (sc2tog, sc 15(14,13)) repeat 5 times total, sc2tog, sc 6(5,4).
Rnd 12: sc 12, (sc2tog, sc 14(13,12)) repeat 5 times total, sc2tog, sc 2(1,0).
Rnd 13: (sc2tog, sc 13(12,11) repeat 6 times total.
Rnd 14: sc 3, (sc2tog, sc 12(11,10)) repeat 5 times total, sc2tog, sc 9(8,7).
Rnd 15: sc 6, (sc2tog, sc 11(10,9)) repeat 5 times total, sc2tog, sc 5(4,3).
Rnd 16: (sc2tog, sc 10(9,8)) repeat 6 times total.
Rnd 17: sc 1, (sc2tog, sc 9(8,7)) repeat 5 times total, sc2tog, sc 8(7,6).
Rnd 18: sc 4, (sc2tog, sc 8(7,6)) repeat 5 times total, sc2tog, sc 4(3,2).
Rnd 19: (sc2tog, sc 7(6,5)) repeat 6 times total.
Rnd 20: sc 4, (sc2tog, sc 6(5,4)) repeat 5 times total, sc2tog, sc 2(1,0).
Rnd 21: sc 1, (sc2tog, sc 5(4,3)) repeat 5 times total, sc2tog, sc 4(3,2).
Rnd 22: sc 1, (sc2tog, sc 4(3,2)) repeat 5 times total, sc2tog, sc 2(1,0).
Rnd 23: (sc2tog, sc 3(2,1)) repeat 6 times total.
For size small skip the next two rounds.
Rnd 24: (sc2tog, sc 2(1)) repeat 6 times total.
For size medium skip the next round.
Rnd 25: (sc2tog, sc 1) repeat 6 times total.
For all sizes:
Rnd 26: sc2tog around ending with 6 stitches total, fasten off leaving a 6 inch tail.

Weave the yarn end through every other stitch and pull tight to close off the hole. Fasten off and hide the yarn end.
Now flip the hat over and working along the bottom of the hat and crocheting on the
bottom black border:
Attach your black yarn to the lower right side of the triangle. You will be working in
rounds with a join for this part.
Rnd 1: sc 30 along the bottom of the triangle, sc 60(54,48) along the bottom of your
starting chain for round 1 of the hat. Join with a slip stitch to the 1st sc, ch 1, do not turn.
Rnd 2-3: sc in same stitch as your slip stitch, sc around, join with a slip stitch to the first sc, ch 1.
Woking two fpdc rows:
Row 4: fpdc around the first st, fpdc 59(53,47), ch 1, turn.
Row 5: fpdc around each fpdc, fasten off leaving a 24 inch tail.
Fold the last two fpdc rows up and sew the top to the first round of red in the hat. Fasten off.

Buttons: Make two.
Rnd 1: Using magic loop method, sc 6. Pull tight to make a circle.
Rnd 2: 2 sc in each stitch around.
Fasten off leaving a 6 inch tail.
Sew one button to the right side of the border just at the end of the fpdc stitches and the other in the same spot on the left side.

Brim: Make two.
Row 1: ch 10, 2 sc in the second chain from hook, sc 7, 2 sc in last chain, ch 1, turn.
Row 2: 2 sc in second chain from hook, 2 sc in next chain, sc 7, (2 sc in next ch) twice, ch 1, turn.
Row 3: 2 sc in first sc, sc 2, 2 sc in next sc, sc 7, 2 sc in next sc, sc 2, 2 sc in last sc, ch 1, turn.

Row 4: 2 sc in first sc, sc 4, 2 sc in next sc, sc 7, 2 sc in next sc, sc 4, 2 sc in last sc, ch 1, turn.
Row 5: 2 sc in first sc, sc 6, 2 sc in next sc, sc 7, 2 sc in next sc, sc 6, 2 sc in last sc, ch 1, turn.
Row 6: 2 sc in first sc, sc 8, 2 sc in next sc, sc 7, 2 sc in next sc, sc 8, 2 sc in last sc, ch 1, turn.
Row 7: 2 sc in first sc, sc 10, 2 sc in next sc, sc 7, 2 sc in next sc, sc 10, 2 sc in last sc, ch 1, turn.
Row 8: 2 sc in first sc, sc 12, 2 sc in next sc, sc 7, 2 sc in next sc, sc 12, 2 sc in last sc, ch 1, turn.
Row 9: 2 sc in first sc, sc 14, 2 sc in next sc, sc 7, 2 sc in next sc, sc 14, 2 sc in last sc, ch 1, turn.
Row 10: 2 sc in first sc, sc 16, 2 sc in next sc, sc 7, 2 sc in next sc, sc 16, 2 sc in last sc,
ch 1, turn.
Fasten off when done with the first brim but when done with the second ch 1 but do not cut your yarn. Place the first brim on top of the second and single crochet around the edge by single crocheting through the top and the bottom single crochet stitches at the same time, this fastens the two brim pieces together for a sturdy brim.. Fasten off leaving at least a 12" tail. Place the brim centered in the front of the hat and sew in place.

Emblem:
For the center circle:
Rnd 1: using magic loop method, sc 6, pull tight to close the loop.
Rnd 2: 2 sc in each sc around.
Rnd 3: slip stitch in each sc around. Fasten off leaving a 6 inch tail.
For the long triangle:
Row 1: ch 16, sc in second ch from hook, sc 10, sc2tog, ch 1, turn. (Leaving the last two chains unworked.)
Row 2: sc2tog, sc 5, sc2tog, ch 1, turn.
Row 3: sc2tog, sc 2, sc2tog, ch 1, turn.
Row 4: sc2tog twice. Do not ch 1, or turn.
Begin single crocheting around the outside of the emblem by single crocheting around the last stitch of row ends and single crocheting in each

unworked stitch along the side of the triangle, 2 single crochets in the corner, single crochet across the top along the back of the starting chain, 2 single crochets in the corner, single crochet in each unworked single crochet and in each row end along the last side of the triangle. Fasten off leaving at least a 12 inch tail. Place the center circle on top of the triangle and use the tail from the circle to sew it in place. Place the emblem onto the hat in the center front and sew into place. Hide all yarn ends and enjoy.

Tyrant Helm

Materials needed:
- Size g or 4.25mm crochet hook
- 3 oz Worsted weight yarn in Light Blue or main color of your choice
- 2.5 oz Worsted weight yarn in Tan
- 1 oz Worsted weight yarn in White
- 5 yds Worsted weight yarn of each Black and Gray. (can also use a chunky gray for buttons)
- 10g of stuffing.

Gauge: 4 fpdc + 4 rows = 1 inch

Measurements: This hat measures 23" around at the base, and 8" from top of hat to bottom.

Abbreviations:
ch – chain
st(s) – stitch(es)
sc – single crochet
sc2tog – single crochet two together
dc – double crochet
fpdc – front post double crochet
bpdc – back post double crochet
slst – slip stitch
rnd – round

Note: Joins are worked as - slst into first actual stitch of the round. Work first stitch in the same stitch as slip stitch.

Working main part of helm first:
Increasing 6 sts per round -
Rnd 1: ch 1, 6 sc in second ch from hook, join. (6 sts)
Rnd 2: ch 1, (sc, fpdc around same stitch) around, join. (12 sts)
Rnd 3: ch 1, (sc, fpdc around same stitch, fpdc) around, join. (18 sts)
Rnd 4: ch 1, (sc, fpdc around same stitch, 2 fpdc) around, join. (24 sts)

Rnd 5: ch 1, (sc, fpdc around same stitch, 3 fpdc) around, join. (30 sts)
Increasing 5 sts per round -
Rnd 6: ch 1, (sc, fpdc around same stitch, 5 fpdc) around, join. (35 sts)
Rnd 7: ch1, (sc, fpdc around same stitch, 6 fpdc) around, join. (40 sts)
Continue in this way, increasing 5 sts per round for 10 more rows.
There will be 85 sts total.
Rnd 17-26: ch 1, fpdc around, join. (85 fpdc)
Change to tan colored yarn.
Rnd 27-31: ch 1, sc around, join.
Rnd 32: ch 1, fpdc around, join.
Rnd 33-36: ch 1, bpdc around, join. Fasten off.
Your helmet will look like Image 1 below.

Image 1

Image 2

Turn the hat right side up and flip the last five rnds up to form the bottom of the hat (Image 2).
Sew the top of rnd 36 into place on the hat.

Tan strip from front to back around center of helm:
Row 1: ch 53 with tan yarn, dc in third ch from hook and all chains across, ch 1, turn. (50 dc)
Row 2: bpdc across, ch 1, turn. (50 sts)
Row 3: fpdc across, ch 1, turn.
Row 4: bpdc across, ch 1, turn.

Row 5: fpdc across, ch 1, turn. Fasten off.
Lay this strip over the top of the hat, from top of the tan in center front, to top of tan in center back, sew into place.

Full horn (right side horn):
ch 30 with tan yarn, join with slst to first ch.
Rnd 1: ch 2, dc around, join. (30 sts)
Rnd 2-3: ch 1, fpdc around, join.
Fasten off.

Join white to top of rnd 2 of tan, from the inside of the ring just made.

Rnd 1: sc around the top of fpdcs, join. (30 sts)

Rnd 2: ch 1, sc around, join. (30 sts)

Now there will be six short rows as follows:
Row 1: ch 1, sc2tog, sc to last four sts, ch 1, turn. (25 sts)
Row 2: sc2tog, sc to within the last three stitches of row, ch 1, turn. (21 sts)
Row 3: sc2tog, sc to last three sts, ch 1, turn. (17 sts)
Row 4: sc2tog, sc to last three sts, ch 1, turn. (13 sts)
Row 5: sc2tog, sc to last three sts, ch 1, turn. (9 sts)
Row 6: sc2tog, sc to last three sts, ch 1, turn. (5 sts)

Your horn will look like Image 3 below.
Row 7: (Picking up stitches and working back to round end) sc2tog, sc 3, sc in corner, sc 3, sc in corner, sc 3, sc in corner, sc 2, sc2tog, join. (16 sts)
Your horn will look like Image 4 below.

Image 3

Image 4

Now working in the round again, and picking up stitches from short rows as follows:
Rnd 3: sc 3, sc in corner, sc 3, sc in corner, sc 3, sc in corner, sc to rnd end, join. (28 sts)
Rnd 4: ch 1, sc around, join. (28 sts)
Rnd 5: ch 1, sc2tog, sc to last two sts, sc2tog, join. (26 sts)

Work six more short rows:
Row 1-5: repeat previous rows 1-5 of the last short row section.
Row 6: sc 2, ch1, turn.
Row 7: (Again picking up stitches and working back to round end) sc 2, sc in corner, sc 3, sc in corner, sc 3, sc in corner, sc 1, sc 2, join, ch1. (14 sts)

Repeat Rnd 3 and 4. (24 sts)
Rnd 3: sc 3, sc in corner, sc 3, sc in corner, sc 3, sc in corner, sc to rnd end. (24 sts)
Rnd 6-8: ch 1, sc2tog, sc to last two sts, sc2tog, join. (18 sts at end of rnd 8)

Change to black.

Rnd 8: ch 1, sc2tog, sc to last two sts, sc2tog, join. (16 sts)
Rnd 9: ch 1, sc2tog, sc to last two sts, sc2tog, join. (14 sts)
Rnd 10: ch 1, sc2tog, sc to last two sts, sc2tog, join. (12 sts)
Rnd 11: ch 1, sc2tog, sc to last two sts, sc2tog, join. (10 sts)
Rnd 12: ch 1, sc2tog, sc to last two sts, sc2tog, join. (8 sts)
Rnd 13: ch 1, sc2tog, sc to last two sts, sc2tog, join. (6 sts)
Rnd 14: ch 1, sc2tog, sc to last two sts, sc2tog, join.

Break yarn, weave around sts and pull through the center. Stuff this horn and sew it to the right side of the hat, in the center of the blue section.

Broken horn (left side horn):
Follow instructions as for the right side horn for Rnds 1-3 of the tan sections and Rnd 1 and 2 of the white section. There should be 30 sts.
Now you will crochet 4 points around this ring, working in rows, as follows:

With white:
Section 1:
Row 1: sc 6, sc2tog, ch 1, turn.
Row 2: sc2tog, sc 2, sc2tog, ch 1, turn.
Row 3: sc2tog twice, fasten off.
Section 2:
Reattach white yarn to the next unworked stitch of rnd 3.
Row 1: sc2tog, sc 6, sc2tog, ch 1, turn.
Row 2: sc 6, sc2tog, ch 1, turn.
Row 3: sc2tog, sc 3, sc2tog, ch 1, turn.
Row 4: sc 3, sc2tog, ch 1, turn.

Row 5: sc2tog twice, fasten off.
Section 3:
Work as for section 1.
Section 4:
Reattach white yarn to the next unworked stitch of rnd 3.
Row 1: sc2tog twice, ch 1, turn.
Row 2: sc2tog, fasten off.

Reattach white yarn to the first stitch of section 1 and sc one round along the tops of all sections with one sc in all single crochets and one single crochet in all corners. Fasten off.

Inside ring: (Either magic loop or chain can be used in Rnd 1)
Rnd 1: With white yarn, ch 2, sc 6 in second ch from hook, do not join, place marker. (6 sts)
Rnd 2: 2 scs in each sc around. (12 sts)
Rnd 3: (sc, 2 sc in next st) around. (18 sts)
Rnd 4: (sc 2, 2 sc in next st) around. (24 sts)
Rnd 5: (2 sc, sc 3) around. (30 sts)
Fasten off.
Sew to the inside of the broken horn, just under the first white rnd.
Stuff the bottom of the horn and sew onto the left side of the hat, in the center of the blue section.

Buttons: (make 10)
Rnd 1: Magic loop, sc 5, pull tight, join. Break yarn.
Sew these to the bottom of the hat, around the tan section evenly spaced.
Hide tails and enjoy your work.

Nappers Respite

Materials:
Main color (cc) – 6 oz. Red heart worsted weight yarn in black
Contrasting color (mc) – 6 oz. Red heart worsted weight yarn in red
1 oz. Red heart worsted weight yarn in white for the ball
Size G or 4.25 mm crochet hook
Yarn needle

Gauge: 4 rows + 4 sc = 1 inch

Abbreviations:
ch: chain
sc(s): single crochet(s)
sc2tog: single crochet two together
st: stitch
rnd: round

Measurements:
small: 18" around,

Note:
This hat is worked flat, in rows and then sewn together. There are four short rows
worked in the center of every stripe then the 6th row of every stripe brings you back to the top. The shape is going to look odd after a few stripes but that is because the bottom 20 sts of the hat will always be flat, when the hat is finished they will be folded up to make the brim.
Also, there is no need to cut the yarn at the end of each stripe when you change color
unless you want to, you can just let it hang out until you need it again and bring it over, there are a lot less ends to hide this way.

With mc ch 41

Row1: sc in second ch from hook and each ch across, there will be 40 scs, ch1, turn.

Row2: sc 35, sc2tog, ch1, turn.
Row3: sc2tog, sc to end, ch1, turn.
Row4: sc 30, sc2tog, ch1, turn.
Row5: sc2tog, sc to end, ch1, turn.
Row6: sc 30, sc 2 along side of short row, sc 3, sc 2 along side of short row, sc 3,
change to cc, ch1, turn.
Begin increasing:
Row7: sc 19, 2 sc in next st, sc to end, ch1, turn.
Row8: sc 35, sc2tog, ch1, turn
Row9: sc2tog, sc 14, 2 sc in next st, sc to end, ch1, turn.
Row10: sc 30, sc2tog, ch1, turn.
Row11: sc2tog, sc 9, 2 sc in next st, sc to end, ch1, turn.
Row12: sc 31, sc 2 along side of short row, sc 4, sc 2 along side of short row, sc 4,
change to mc, ch1, turn.
Row13: sc 22, 2 sc in next st, sc to end, ch1, turn.
Row14: sc 37, sc2tog, ch1, turn.
Row15: sc2tog, sc 16, 2 sc in next st, sc to end, ch1, turn.
Row16: sc 31, sc2tog, ch1, turn.
Row17: sc2tog, sc 10, 2 sc in next st, sc to end, ch1, turn.
Row18: sc 32, sc 2 along side of short row, sc 5, sc 2 along side of short row, sc 5,
change to cc, ch1, turn.
Row19: sc 25, 2 sc in next st, sc to end, ch1, turn.
Row20: sc 39, sc2tog, ch1, turn.
Row21: sc2tog, sc 18, 2 sc in next st, sc to end, ch1, turn.
Row22: sc 32, sc2tog, ch1, turn.
Row23: sc2tog, sc 11, 2 sc in next st, sc to end, ch1, turn.
Row24: sc 33, sc 2 along side of short row, sc 6, 2 sc along side of short row, sc 6,
change to mc, ch1, turn.
Row25: sc 28, 2 sc in next st, sc to end, ch1, turn.
Row26: sc 41, sc2tog, ch1, turn.
Row27: sc2tog, sc 20, 2 sc in next st, sc to end, ch1, turn.

Row28: sc 33, sc2tog, ch1, turn.
Row29: sc2tog, sc 12, 2 sc in next st, sc to end, ch1, turn.
Row30: sc 34, 2 sc along side of short row, sc 7, 2 sc along side of short row, sc 7,
change to cc, ch1, turn.
Row31: sc 31, 2 sc in next st, sc to end, ch1, turn.
Row32: sc 43, sc2tog, ch1, turn.
Row33: sc2tog, sc 22, 2 sc in next st, sc to end, ch1, turn.
Row34: sc 34, sc2tog, ch1, turn.
Row35: sc2tog, sc 13, 2 sc in next st, sc to end, ch1, turn.
Row36: sc 35, 2 sc along side of short row, sc 8, 2 sc along side of short row, sc 8,
change to mc, ch1, turn.
Row37: sc 34, 2 sc in next st, sc to end, ch1, turn.
Row38: sc 45, sc2tog, ch1, turn.
Row39: sc2tog, sc 24, 2 sc in next st, sc to end, ch1, turn.
Row40: sc 35, sc2tog, ch1, turn.
Row41: sc2tog, sc 14, 2 sc in next st, sc to end, ch1, turn.
Row42: sc 36, 2 sc along side of short row, sc 9, 2 sc along side of short row, sc 9,
change to cc, ch1, turn.
End increasing.
Row43: sc to end, ch1, turn.
Row44: sc 47, sc2tog, ch1, turn.
Row45: sc2tog, sc to end, ch1, turn.
Row46: sc 36, sc2tog, ch1, turn.
Row47: sc2tog, sc to end, ch1, turn.
Row48: sc 36, 2 sc along side of short row, sc 9, 2 sc along side of short row, sc 9,
change to mc, ch1, turn.
Row 49-54: Repeat rows 43-48, change to cc, ch1, turn.
Begin decreasing and reverse shaping:
Row55: sc across, ch1, turn.
Row56: sc 20, sc2tog, sc 14, sc2tog, ch1, turn.
Row57: sc2tog, sc to end, ch1, turn.

Row58: sc 20, sc2tog, sc 13, 2 sc along the side of short row, sc 9, sc2tog, ch1, turn.
Row59: sc2tog, sc to end, ch1, turn.
Row60: sc 20, sc2tog, sc 23, 2 sc along the side of short row, sc 9, change to mc, ch1, turn.
Row61: sc across, ch1, turn.
Row62: sc 20, sc2tog, sc 13, sc2tog, ch1, turn.
Row63: sc2tog, sc to end, ch1, turn.
Row64: sc 20, sc2tog, sc 12, 2 sc along the side of short row, sc 8, sc2tog, ch1, turn.
Row65: sc2tog, sc to end, ch1, turn.
Row66: sc 20, sc2tog, sc 21, 2 sc along the side of short row, sc 8, change to cc, ch1, turn.
Row67: sc across, ch1, turn.
Row68: sc 20, sc2tog, sc 12, sc2tog, ch1, turn.
Row69: sc2tog, sc to end, ch1, turn.
Row70: sc 20, sc2tog, sc 11, 2 sc along the side of short row, sc 7, sc2tog, ch1, turn.
Row71: sc2tog, sc to end, ch1, turn.
Row72: sc 20, sc2tog, sc 19, 2 sc along the side of short row, sc 7, change to mc, ch1, turn.
Row73: sc across, ch1, turn.
Row74: sc 20, sc2tog, sc 11, sc2tog, ch1, turn.
Row75: sc2tog, sc to end, ch1, turn.
Row76: sc 20, sc2tog, sc 10, 2 sc along the side of short row, sc 6, sc2tog, ch1, turn.
Row77: sc2tog, sc to end, ch1, turn.
Row78: sc 20, sc2tog, sc 17, 2 sc along the side of short row, sc 6, change to cc, ch1, turn.
Row79: sc across, ch1, turn.
Row80: sc 20, sc2tog, sc 10, sc2tog, ch1, turn.
Row81: sc2tog, sc to end, ch1, turn.
Row82: sc 20, sc2tog, sc 9, 2 sc along the side of short row, sc 5, sc2tog, ch1, turn.
Row83: sc2tog, sc to end, ch1, turn.

Row84: sc 20, sc2tog, sc 15, 2 sc along the side of short row, sc 5, change to mc, ch1, turn.
Row85: sc across, ch1, turn.
Row86: sc 20, sc2tog, sc 9, sc2tog, ch1, turn.
Row87: sc2tog, sc to end, ch1, turn.
Row88: sc 20, sc2tog, sc 8, 2 sc along side of shor row, sc 4, sc2tog, ch1, turn.
Row89: sc2tog, sc to end, ch1, turn.
Row90: sc 20, sc2tog, sc 15, 2 sc along the side of short row, sc 4, change to cc, ch1, turn.
End decreasing.
Row91: sc across, ch1, turn.
Row92: sc 30, sc2tog, ch1, turn.
Row93: sc2tog, sc to end, ch1, turn.
Row94: sc 30, 2 sc along the side of short row, sc 3, sc2tog, ch1, turn.
Row95: sc2tog, sc to end, ch1, turn.
Row96: sc 35, 2 sc along the side of short row, sc 3, ch1.
Cut the ends of both yarns leaving a 6 inch tail for one and about a 24 inch tail for the other, (one to weave in the top and one to sew along the side) weave the 6 inch tail along the end of every other row twice and pull tight and fasten off to finish off the top.
With the other yarn end, make sure the wrong side of the hat is facing out, sew the first row and the last row of the hat together only until you have the last 20 sts left, then flip the hat right side out and finish sewing up the seam. Now fold the bottom half of the brim up. Hide yarn ends.
For the ball: worked in the round without joins.
Using the magic loop method-
Rnd1: Sc 6 in loop, pull tight.
Rnd2: 2 sc in each st around. (12 sc)
Rnd3: (sc 1, 2 sc in next st) repeat around. (18 sc)
Rnd4: (sc 2, 2 sc in next st) repeat around. (24 sc)
Rnd5-7: sc around. (24 sc)
Rnd8: (sc 2, sc2tog) around. (18 sc)
Rnd9: (sc 1, sc2tog) around. (12 sc)
Leaving a 12 inch tail, cut yarn and fasten off.

Using the tail from the ball sew it to the tip of the hat, fasten off and hide all remaining yarn ends.

Craft Bindings

Print, Bind, Ship - Printing Services
Custom Notebooks, Planners and Workbooks
Photo Cover Notebooks, Planners and Workbooks
Knit and Crochet Pattern Book Shop
Knitting and Crocheting Pattern Instant Downloads

All at CraftBindings.com!
Join our Customer Loyalty Program and start receiving discounts right away!
- Gift Cards Also Available -

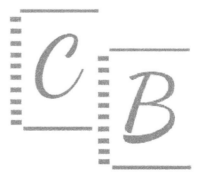

craftbindings.com

www.ingramcontent.com/pod-product-compliance
Lightning Source LLC
Chambersburg PA
CBHW081423231224
19429CB00031B/219